Free Verse Editions

Edited by Jon Thompson

Divination Machine

F. Daniel Rzicznek

Parlor Press
West Lafayette, Indiana
www.parlorpress.com

Parlor Press LLC, West Lafayette, Indiana 47906

Printed in the United States of America
S A N: 2 5 4 - 8 8 7 9

Library of Congress Cataloging-in-Publication Data

Rzicznek, F. Daniel (Frank Daniel), 1979-
Divination machine / F. Daniel Rzicznek.
    p. cm. -- (Free verse editions)
ISBN 978-1-60235-118-9 (pbk. : alk. paper) -- ISBN 978-1-
    60235-119-6 (adobe ebook)
I. Title.
PS3618.Z53D58 2009
811'.6--dc22
                                        2009032566

Cover design: Frank Cucciarre, Blink Concept & Design, Inc.
Printed on acid-free paper.

Parlor Press, LLC is an independent publisher of scholarly
and trade titles in print and multimedia formats. This book
is available in paper and Adobe eBook formats from Parlor
Press on the World Wide Web at http://www.parlorpress.
com or through online and brick-and-mortar bookstores.
For submission information or to find out about Parlor Press
publications, write to Parlor Press, 816 Robinson St., West
Lafayette, Indiana, 47906, or e-mail editor@parlorpress.com.

for Amanda

Contents

Contents

Acknowledgments

Gratitude is due to the editors of the following publications in which some of these poems (sometimes in slightly different form) first appeared: *Barn Owl Review, Barnstorm, Boston Review, Del Sol Review, Free Verse, Front Porch, The Greensboro Review, Harpur Palate, The Literary Review, Margie, The New Republic, Parthenon West Review, Poet Lore, Rhino*, and *Runes: A Review of Poetry*. The two epigraphs that begin this collection are from *Manual of Zen Buddhism* by D. T. Suzuki (Grove Press, 1960) and *The Deep North* by Fanny Howe (Sun & Moon Press, 1991).

Thank you to my family and friends, near and far, and to the Wick Poetry Center at Kent State University as well as both the Creative Writing Program and the General Studies Writing Program at Bowling Green State University for their continued encouragement and support. Thanks to the poets who have given their comments and reactions to these poems over the last few years, and thanks also to the following individuals who read this work in manuscript form: John Freeman, Mark Jenkins, Matt McBride, Gary L. McDowell, Amy Newman, Christof Scheele, and Larissa Szporluk. Thanks to Djelloul Marbrook and H.L. Hix for their generous words and thanks to Frank Cuccairre for his vision and patience. Thanks also to Jon Thompson and David Blakesley. Loving thanks to Amanda, for rescuing me.

Divination Machine

"If anyone should ask the meaning of this,
Behold the lilies of the field and its fresh sweet-scented verdure."

—Pu-Ming, translated by D.T. Suzuki

"All answers are hells."

—Fanny Howe

Blueprint

I know this can continue.
Even if allowed to speak
with the forest's dark stations
for ten hundred million years—

even if the shadowed, jagged
wings of scavengers convince me
of blood's speed and the reiteration
of matter through belief

in reiteration. Even when
a late train pounds haggardly
out through the marshlands
before plunging into woods

and my limbs know themselves
one at a time in the night
among the lists of leaves, how some
are sharp: needles and blades,

how others are only notions
wedding their fanned, star-pointed
structures six months out
of twelve. Yes: blood's speed

and the reoccurrence of nativity—
a someone walks into the trees, alone.
Inside that view a *you* forms.
Swiftly, think back: a dare—a *we*.

Cost of Living

Dear Ancestor: I have learned to smell arteries of coal
when they are but hundreds of miles away.
The rivers here hold many forms
that perish daily, whether the people care or not.
I have learned to grow fur.
The birds fear me less.

~

You say the adage
of every machine must be math:
rise of red, nausea of combustion and wind.

Your own sleeping breath
on your own arm
sleeps like smothered wildflowers.

Your eyes search inward for a burrow
or at least a flat plot of ground
in which to dig. The god of steam-power

be thanked, the goals of market be blessed.

~

What's more meaningful than the names and lines,
the map's shadings and various pastels,
is the shadow cast on the dash

where you scan the land, where
the red needle follows your eyebrows up.
Someone else is driving you.

~

If we want to talk about life
then the first word to mention is *meat*.
A good blade can take one a long way.

~

Dear Ancestor: the people are no longer interested
in the way their bones ascend
through petal and leaf. In equating horses
with power they have sent light
and noise barreling through the old dark
of woods and open hills. So much
for the infinite beauty of consciousness.

I'm coming home.

Machine Visions

My body a fast jade branch
in the riverbed. In the underground
the ants' plum-black kingdom,
constructing. Headwaters: thoughts
resurrecting in vapors, in waves.
Alphabet of sandhill cranes, snail
alphabet, gut alphabet. My body
a tendril of corn in the field's teeth.
All growing things, all things
of before tasted in them. The ants
ascending my door—evening's
half-formed face. The trees swift
as wings, green as thoughtlessness.
The dogs black through rain, the dogs
brown in sun. Mountain island:
a phrase to confuse the self outright.
The worm feels the night with
the whole of its body, ascends.
Spring come reeling back to me,
spring come reeling back to me.
Never the same, this raining—
my body a northern pike stick-still
in olive water under ancient pines.
Acorns in the wood duck's craw,
acorns bobbing on the river. Moon
faces downward, upward—what of
worship? What of amnesia?
My body a brightened thing falling
stroke after stroke after stroke on
the list of glowing, perfect things.
The world spins off into the world:
groan of winter wolves beneath
the chimney's morning banner,
the lock's cold click behind the door,
weeds suddenly taller than the sky.

Thicket

In the dream, myself
and a faceless stranger determine
that language (as suspected earlier
in a dim, blood-caked diner) does not
exist. Therefore (we concluded)
poetry is a paranormal event,
and then I woke, choking
on a rope of light that, as it uncoiled
through my mouth, sent scouts of air
around the house. I led myself
to the coffee, studied the detailed mug:

the hairline cracks trees caused
across the moon and water, the leaves
lost and clinging to the feet of oaks,
the old truck grown cold
since the day's ride into the valley,
the canoe upside down on sawhorses,
spruces hugging the chimney's
stonework. Who leaves a shotgun
by the door, let alone two, and likely
loaded? What geese coast through woods
and just yards above the obvious cabin?
I found myself there, answering:

I love the river, where it laps in
to make the dock a thing of use. I covet
the ladder, the little nowhere it leads to.

Crow Station

To be gone and not to rest—
to work and to work and to work.

To feel blood sculpt (cold
as slate) around reality, sapping

essential night, and the birds there:
beautiful and plucking gifts

from the dead. One hand still
gestures skyward, flesh

blown back from bone, like foam—
sea rushing on land.

~

No visions last night—no trees,
no songs for them. Out:

the furnace and its boulders
spasmodic in the home's underworld,

how windows must be heaven
above it all (paint husk, wolf spiders)

with those shriven maples gaunt
over splotched lawns, dry streets, as if

I in the dirt am remembering,
detail on detail, speaking of it.

The microscopic scripture returns—
smallest boat in any world.

Overhanging branches—the way
in which the throngs of the dead

describe what remains they
can still see of the land above.

All salt. All salt and light. Birdnoise.
All birdnoise. The scripture

drifts past unnoticed, curled
inward like a fortune.

Where the trail switched, closed
in behind me like an army,

was not found in the dream, only
the dry riverbed in winter.

And somehow I scrawled
the terms of it on my ceiling (I

was outside, beneath the ice-white sky—
I was asleep in the room…)

The cars zipping there on the road,
those hearts catapulted toward the sea.

Absolutely the sky's pied breasts
dip nearly grass-level and the air

inside one: a thousand creased faces.
(Hold back, hold tight, bite down,

that first thought can betray.)
Lord, how the dead carry

on all night in the impassable tunnels
of a turning sleep—the beat

hot as rain pocking rust
in the ear's dock, the pillow darkening.

And what of the body's day-long list?
(The body in cells, start to finish.)

I turn from it as from a carved wall,
a wall carved with deeds,

thoughts long (day-long) drowned.
The wall with me, the wall burning

but unconsumed, the wall tall
now as my body, all cells

from egg to worm, all cells upward—
all that I have done.

Hulking pines lean apart, as if
some monster wind had stumbled

through. Dark canoes tilt empty
to the ashy bank. Fog distrupts

the facing shore. (A crow breaks it.)
What seam in the journey

came unsewn? (A crow peeling
back the scalp.) What message

stands delayed in my blood?
(A crow laughing at the river.)

~

So the body prays this way, reborn:
a traveler on foot, picking

a zigzag line through mountains.
The hours elongate between

last blood and afterlife, the chatter
of gravel, the robe of sleet

hung from a cloud for me.
I mapped the mountain slopes

and the manuscript evaporated.
I walked into a burning world.

And I followed the molting swan
(who screamed, but gently, and into

the spring underbrush) until I lost
her, which was the first moment.

But the purple, tremoring bundles
of thistle emerging, the scent

of living water. How did I go up
and under at once? How

the ragged, golden uplands flowing
westward, miraculous, beneath me?

Storm King

Dusk plummets—a numb anger
behind the tidal screens
of corn, the day's noise
haunting the sanguine ridges

in the throats of animals
so quick and plain I can tell
what they are from the pine
I sway in. The coyotes

harbor fur and trample by
on all fours. The pine's sage lace
thickens its sap in the unshored
light. The living

with their windowed eyes lick
the angles of wilderness:
where the beech meets the row,
where under the soybeans

a fossil asleep does not recall
its welded eye—does not hear
the little, electric curse
I mutter toward the town.

Evening: Disorder

The sidewalk home (sundown path)
I feel perception grinding into,
messenger that forgets, always,
by the gasp of arrival,
                            what vision
(yellow sky—blue sky) it meant
for me: the winter dirt of houses,
the sapling, snapped by some drunks
            at its base, pointing north
on someone's lawn.
                            Everything
is a piece of the vision: say
I look up from a book and night
has fallen—say a robe sewn
from willows, with extreme care
is less than what's required,
                            so much
less that the need for morning
            dries up. How I see the world,
how I can't stop from seeing it,
how the world is taken with itself
to the point
            of sickness:
the squeak of my chair's rollers
I hear as geese over the rooftop,
the phone rings with the unknown
stationed firmly ahead of it,
            the sideways ache
of a full bladder the body forgets,
for just an instant, what to do with.

Say I glance up
              a second time;
night is still there (black as a kite
stuck in a summer tree for so long
that once the leaves descend one
         over one, it hangs still, winter
returning to knock it loose
from bare branches,
                        its spot on the lawn
like a shadow trapped when others
have lifted, a deep, persistent patch
on the already darkened ground)…

Alewife

To cure:

let ache turn your sight
in circles. Let

a ghost through that door.

The speck of vatic dust runs
blind to leaves

that kneel, bask yellow.

Let that late soul the ghost
enter and enter:

the spirals of fish

through which the sea's air
is every second resurrected.

River Enough

Nothing happened today.
The nearest big water waits
outside town. I have half
a mind to shrink into the forest
and grow rusty with minutes.

What in it, in the clean glint
as viewed from behind trees,
can resist the mind's tiny catalog
and its insistent naming, even
when each view slides to fit
the notion of a larger movement:

great river the color of stasis,
the new slinks of current it joins?
The time it takes to blacken
a box of the calendar is enough
to turn me around: the days
passing lightly through me—me,
a rush of tributary eating snow.

Ice Bed: Visions

It seems the mountains
      switch places overnight.

A flush of snow partridge:
      a vanishing into vanishing.

The oak where bees
      toss their dead to the ground.

The freeze-whitened treelimb:
      the glass-encased treelimb.

The sun and its roof
      of blood: heavy light of cold.

The copper owl with a green
      bone in his beak. In the world's

basement: faint drip
      that drowns and drowns.

Thicket

The lightest of rains pins me.
The *what* of *must happen*, eye blooming
(not the *will*) before the sun
and wings stretched through with wire,
how they hold the hawk to the fence
flowing apart, icy as blood
where the circuit has run its length.
I have ignored the sanctum
of leafless trees, dragged a skipjack
from beach to butcher, flapping
madly as he was by the tail.
Let me tell you about my day:

the lightest of rains pins me
and the smallest of ceremonies: sleep,
those horns of dust sounding miles
down in the ear, and who's to measure
the endlessness of such dark, even
with the orrery of uncast winters
spinning, a chandelier to guide us?

Light before Daybreak

A freezing mist halves the marsh
and I am a voice half asleep
in a hollowed tree.
                I am but a voice.
Not the gathering quickness of rats.
Not a lion's green skull floating
through the dry heights of grass.

A voice: click and drawl that trails
behind the walking lights,
                     but I
have nothing for electric light, though
I am half worshipful of stars here,
their queasy belts of silver tied
across the pine-toothed horizon.

I am roused and mingle instantly
with far bootsteps and the cries
of two crows above the gravel lane.

I ensnare bootsteps and some skinny
lengths of metal, and a panting thing
tearing the reeds.
              Not the men
and not their dogs, barely the sounds
they toss with less than a thought
into water. I am a fallen line
of fenceposts finally evaporating
in the sun. I am a low hum
behind the wind:

           what the hunters hear
as they snap awake midday, the bronze
water a tide between their ears,
when I wish I could bless them all.

Far

The river had peddled here months,
waiting (it froze only once
this winter—oaks silver
with wind, the dogs of my feet
sore from road and stone, left

like bones beneath the table (I sit,
wide window on my left,

river hollering its uneven body
of sand and shrouds, what's left

after snow, after windburn, what bristles
(voices caught in the pitfall,
what the veined, moss-bright skull
of a cabbage emits as it loosens
on the lawn, raucous blue jays
tugging at the leafy membrane,
birds that a month ago had left

(warmth to the north too loud
to resist, and that day I
had set out from these calm hills
through rain, toward home—
the river my companion, my accuser,
slow guide, fog's visual clamor
like a compass in dusk, fog intoxicated
with its own edge (tracks left

where others had deepened their lungs
and crossed lightly into sense.

Natural: History

In the collection of mammals
the dead elk are given dust and some shrubs

and pines to freeze with, to hold
    raw antlers above.

The diorama behind them: red curve
of plow creasing a wheat field, vultures

hung in threes like bells behind the mountain flutes
    and narrating voice.

Slow fingers disarm the tour mid-habitat,
quiet the lights to orange.

The day's last footfalls fade, and the moment
    sends one elk's head

into reflection: snout, neck, eyes inventing
a pedestal. If there were a looking from out

of the eyes, it could awake through this,
    but the world

in all its difficult cycles, is missing:
wind, snow, blood, rot, rain, change.

Doctor of Maps

One version scrawled at dusk
on the sky's surrounding edge

has the wounded hawk slipping
whole again from the yard,
a scar of grass sealing the soil,
the streetlights shaping a pool

for the wing's shadow to begin
and the only noise I know
while kneeling there in the scene

(bird half awake, my eyes
                              a force
averted into dirt)

is a car's gray laughter
and the low crackle of tires like fire
chewing paper. I would mention
details from the flowerbed—

I would say the petals
could last a week into winter
if this version would allow me
a task other than the hawk
and its birth from the lawn,

the low roar of earth giving
out with a shiver through street,
town, country, and continent.

I am called away to the place
where I already am, the hawk
granting me one slack thought:

the tall chimney, the way
the smoke gathers, slithers back in.

Plea

The apology arrives swift
and slow, like roses
rotting toward spring—

the apology eats wind
for wood and burns
the first frost off,
snow without water

equaling the air's ward,
equaling the apology one
face tells another:
one ruined mood
lifting into the trees,

their leaves bending
the invisible autumn
into an apology left
there, between earth

and leaf before falling,
the apology leveling
gravity with a hush—

the apology rattling
the roofs of lovers,
drawing them from sleep
like music with legs,
takes one by the shoulder

and turns her, turns
her hands to a window
to check the lock,
the apology there a squeak:

the noise arcing out
where it wakes a sparrow
who thinks, for a moment,
that morning has come.

Nightjournal

A story I've never heard: a man's wish
to be burned at death, his ashes
stewed with pulp to make a book
on the flightlessness of certain birds.
The dead are no longer the dead—
not even a scattering
of chipped teeth through grass.

~

Starlight number, starlight number:
the earth's cannon points everywhere
for I am exploding. The fish
beneath the skin thrums its dorsal,
flexes its veil. Little threads
of my beard fall away past the mirror.
Only my face remains submerged.

~

A few leaves catch in my skull,
a briar flies from my tongue.
Confessing to a dream is confessing
only to an act imagined
when imagination has a mind of wind,
when rain takes a peony apart,
scatters it down into beauty.

Thicket

The forest is white with the month,
blank as an acre of rain.

The brief tale in which the mind
sews a pasture out of timber,
fescue writhing day on day higher,
the cattle meant for meat released
to fill their bellies with sky and earth.
The mind in the mean time invents
a blade to be swung, a hook to sink.
The fescue rises taller and lower
depending on the year, the cattle
milling in shade or resting under clouds,
the mind killing them now and then
until the day a train flows past.
Saplings uproot the pasture, limbs
growing dense as the decades roll
where cattle and fescue thrived.

The forest is white with the month,
blank as an acre of rain.

Onus

We pass and pass like cloud
through the harp's clean strings,
like scythes of shade curling
in the place an angel occupied—
the bottoms of her feet

shrinking upward, messages
that surface on the other side
of what we struggle beneath:
the way trees through night
shine dark as the river, the road,

and a few breathed words
ring like stars in our rooms
where we calculate our load
of one, where one is multiplied
against our spines and organs.

We pass and pass and pass—
nostril to loam, fingers blue
as slate. We walk to the end,
fall nameless from fraying maps.
Weather tugs our ears shut

like windows on a tossing ship
where glowing gowns ascend
and sing, and sing forever
and know only passage. We stay
aground. We are not sorry.

Rote

Every
morning. Every morning
the sun rolls out
from the hills. Every

morning the old sun rolls sideways out
from the worn hills, sheds
its yellows. Every morning the old sun
rolls sideways like a dial

out from the worn hills, sheds
its yellow rafters
into the brook. Every morning
the sun rolls sideways,
sheds its yellow rafters

into the slow-running brook
(the smallest of acts reinvented,
perpetually *there*) to be caught, tossed
into returning, the yellow light
shedding out, sideways
like a dial in the worn rafters of morning,
in the old, slow-running current of the hills.

Daylight: April

In the kitchen's brightness, naked,
weighing an apple, you came
to me, glasses on, your skin

cooling in the breeze. My list
for the day: a few hornets awake,
re-existing in the air, a car up

on a rusty jack: its crutch,
and then the beautiful socket
where the wheel had spun.

Other parts of the list: the space
between your gums and fingers
where the brick-red apple fit,

filling its own form. The dull eyes
of traffic lights at dusk, a voice
sobbing behind a thin door.

If this slow world were catching
up with itself, I would tell
you something impure, but today

it poured for three minutes
and the weatherman told us
that tomorrow would be all

rain, and I could see the trees
(the stretch of their buds all week)
in explosion, bestowing shade.

Inner Crowd

We stumble into memory and before
we recognize the gate, we are half
    way through, and there are two does

leaping through the high tangles of marsh
and the buck stands
                staring out at us:

our tall shadows, the mind inside the mind
that he can hear
            rumbling above the wind,
even as he disappears into the brush.

            ~

Three times this morning
              the farmer's dogs
play sadness across the forest's spines—
at first we thought *coyotes*
             then

their whimpers descended, something
half lame as they echoed into the lake—

into the slow circlings of fish.

            ~

The first man to move falls, drives gravel
through his knees, and the woman beside him
sets a small bag of money
              ablaze, the light

revealing a multitude of faces stretching
back toward the one-way door of pleasure.

Natural: Enemy

His world is about anger,
this lone rabbit hunkering in snow,

a blind streetlight aloft above
       him like a prayer he cannot say,

(a rabbit cannot chant…)
a charm he is foolish to,

cautious as he is on the lawn,
       the wide sweep and whitening

that veils like dust over it, like the anger
of this rabbit (thought otherwise soft,

in need) at this season unseasonable
       as rope (cascading from nowhere)

to haul the unwound self to safety,
to leave an empty room throbbing.

This arguer, he lurches into woods:
       is torn apart by owls,

is reimagined as a multitude
and never seen content again.

Glass Bed: Visions

The copper owl knows its calling:
        to drop an egg in the juniper's old rot.

A raft of garbage and cold wind
        with three jaundiced gulls turning above.

Finally, the berries agree to ferment:
        now come months of traffic and stone.

Today the spring pulled up its bed,
        those charming wet blades, and moaned.

Cicadas harden beneath the willows
        and diamonds tussle in the ground.

The ships that ride on less than weather
        send all the crew sinking dumbly under.

The snow-soaked moss plays again
        its wide green signal on the earth.

Thicket

Our breathing in sleep never
synchronizes, and in the forest valley
between each double draw and release
a watchman snuffs his lantern,
sinking the hillsides
into darkness. He does not see us
swaying the trees over his land.

We cannot be seen.

A light that once was a body
loosens its gleam, drops
like a curtain over our walls,
passes through the street.
In a rush, the wind's west fist
rams our house, rattles blinds
and siding until we wake,
then dies into ankle-high grass.
It's so late.
        We wonder who
is breathing once more—who woke
from a dream of waves
and wreckage—who tried
hard to sleep again.

Negative

Keepsake: black and white
of the plains before they were plains—
before *impossible*. Some of the grasses

turn, for an instant, gold, then gradients
of cloud and pumice: the skull color,
the breath of glaciers. This is the original

scene, the seconds in which the foreground
trembles. A blackbird ascends with
the flock. There, each pacing heart

is complicated by the others, each wing
has a number of atoms that tear free
and fall apart on the wind, dispersing.

Wherever

The grainy town spills over
around us: a mammoth oak

still leafless in spring, a man
in paint-smeared clothes

shouldering a wooden ladder
through the shade. *No—not here.*

In the lake's glow, geese migrate
from one green shore to the other.

Portage: a lair of arrivals,
bare threshold of all departure.

No—the one house for rent
crippled from the brightness

of neighbors. The phone
number reversed says: *not here.*

Our eyes blink, returning to us.
Sudden motion and the word *home*

dissolving quick in the throat
while the roads that appear uphill

climb—viperous, swooning—
though the land remains level.

Apollo

A salmon's lichen-green tail
catches in the narrow door
of sight—how quick it is
that notions are pried facet
by facet apart in sleep:

soft, nearly metallic bubbles
flying in the river's traffic.
What led to this view:
the sky a smoke of film
past the water's sore drone

and fish shivering past, blind
to my form, I who had
submerged somehow through
sound, the river a mouth agape
behind stars: my mouth a river

at large in the skull, song
of veins drumming dimly as
rapids downstream. A kingfisher
rockets under after nothing,
nature at once finally human,

my need to surface firing
its pain: a reversed erasure.
In spite of sleep my hand
plunges up for naked roots—
touches sunlight on a wall.

Angelbrains

Inside them, under that dull gloss
of crimson wax, there is just one man
and a bare, rocky field where he
is charged to push, through the night, his plow
of elk antlers, the furrows streaking
in jagged lines behind him, the light
tied to his forehead swinging everywhere
he turns, like the long beak of a bird
prodding among sand and dry weeds
where the far off surf is a low pounding,
seaplants tangled in wet rocks, slip
and return of the world's tongue—

and yes, this is the one world
where inside each impossibility, work
undone waits with absolute patience,
where the moon is whatever color it wants,
where the corners of the field fold
under themselves to make the field
a thing without end, a task
at which the plowman can neither
succeed nor fail, his sweat
becoming the spray from the waves,
his arms the uninhabitable shore,
his footsteps slowly turning the earth.

Huron Vision

The level blade of blue sweeps up
     over the porch rail but only

in the background: gracious
     wavelengths that push landward

from points unthought of…
     (feel the tug in each direction?)

As if stalled in being,
     every last light across Earth

blinks on, then off, at once—
     this figure stands in for nothing

when nothing is elsewhere.
     Everything present: boat's wake

drifting smoke-trails like saints
     up from the lake, to the birches,

crossing calm ferns, green gestures,
     and across the road, thinning

above sagging barns that gnaw
     the sky, spit distances.

Silver: Screen

One day we woke to leaves on every tree,
the flinty memory of where we'd been,
what we'd heard, what aligned out there
past the windows we leave open
as we sleep, the sleep that stirs us
even as we row through it, even as sun
shudders over the dew (how an image
flourishes in the shut eye) and we
meet what we can of the day before time
again suspends, before we empty out.

~

As in the way a crowd accumulates
around the beaming abyss of a baby's face.
As in the way that baby fuses new cells
to existing cells (all the while unknowing
the miracle of minutes around it) until
it looks up, half-grown, into moonlight
or clouds or rafters, knows just what
is meant for it in a lone flash, a single,
burdened instant, an image imagined:
the ring a crowd forms around a coffin.

~

And when messengers finally did arrive
(as if the countryside hills and stones
struck some deal to turn them loose, or
as if a great, passing ship had capsized)
they found the fledgling cities hypnotized,
the dwellers all seated in darkness,
walls swarming with light and carnal color.
The messengers hovered before them, un-
sheathed their massive, oak-dark wings, hung
there as if invisible and ignorant as oxygen.

Over: Night

Blue burns dark—I wake ascending
over Minneapolis, one shred
of dead Henry's tongue moaning

like a storm siren—the avenues
scare into fields which go forever,
forever into the moaning river

until we're airborne—blue stars
and green stars and the moaning
still yellow in the clouds, invisible

as bird ghosts along fencerows—
wary and headlong as music
under which sleek hunger wakes

a hungrier noise (the moaning)
and all of it Henry: all
shuffle and drag and breakdown,

all windblown beard and stars—
I can't remember where his tomb is
(old seconds and bones ascend

to clang on green tin and stone)
but this speck, this moaning
works me instantly outside

in—tendrils entangle the cabin,
tilt the wings toward demon,
a flight of omens swifting through.

Divination

~

My life listens for a place where
the snow leans and melts, runs
down, naked as the bright water
that turns green in the mind.

And where does green
                    leave the mind?
The state shines
            with counties all
                            in shades—
names of towns charging
                            through
            the colors like runoff.

Show me, will you please, where
the waters arise from? Next
to this meadow, this road, above
these roiling woods, a spirit:

a face breathing out the dark.

The clear heat at noon, the cheer
of candles at dusk: the arrowlike
surge of sunfish in the pond
the jogging track lassoes.

The girdle of the highway
and everything
                    that enters
            with it: plastic, bone,
glass, and a thousand faces:
a voice exaggerating
                    about
        ceiling, visibility, etc.

One way to understand
my eyes is by looking through
them, but away from any window.
And the clear heat at noon?

You must build it.

One slow gift the sun leaves
is silence. And in the murk of six
o'clock, night's cloth comes in
from the day's shadow-work.

This is all you have to say
to me? Another way to understand
          my own eyes is
with these two
                    hands I
hold together like torches: one
lighting the other. Days have gone
          by like this.

If I could say aloud my true
name, then the town rabbits
who dart from my steps might
be calmed. And what, then,

would I have to marvel at?

~

The county expands like
a deep guffaw: the edges pushing
like the late, well-worn blooms
when the birds swoop

in on the flies. When the birds
        swoop in on the flies
                                    there
is jubilee—there is sculpture.
        One or two centuries
and all of this should
have been perfect. All
        of this should have been

perfect. Certain questions recoil
against the land. *When is a star
not a star? When do the waters
regain consciousness?* Better

yet: when is a star a star?

~

A little grenache runs
over the lip of the glass. Three
nights and the dream
of gigantic flowers busying

like heads
            through the forest floor
        has not left. In it
I am speechless: the spiral
                            pink
bulb, the positively clitoral
                            form
of each spring daimon whirling.

And what else can there be?
The brown hood of dead needles
splayed, and the notion that
a meadow lurks against my back.

And the far away thrash of water.

The mornings grow cooler
in that warmer way—in that
they are cool, and winter
has ventured into the ocean.

A window makes any sun
                              warmer:
robins, sparrows, a jay—
the town is emptied
        and weather sways the trees.
And what do the trees sway
                              like?
            The trees sway like

legs ascending among rocks, debris—
and the guilt that stings
my neck as it turns to find that
what had followed has vanished.

And new songs arrive.

The rocks of the valley are razors
and I am not yet finished
with their depression, their edges.
Somewhere, from out of the lower

canyons, young girls
clutch haggard photographs
of their fathers,
pausing
in the rubble to stare down
into the shadowed brows,
the military hats
at a tilt.

The looks on the girls' faces pass
up into the sky. Without warning
the forest surrounds me: heavy
and pungent with the universe.

What have you done?

A lulling soreness in the throat
and I wake to clouds pushing
other clouds above the streets.
What a lonely time for the corn,

just taken
            from the soil: deposited
deep in silo's dark.
                    Disembodied:
that's the word I've spoken
            in the past when
                    asked by my self
to illuminate loneliness.

And when was last winter,
again? The eyes I use to see
the world offer little, if any,
homage to that world. Always

I forget I am part of it.

~

I had been speaking about
the way images reflect back
on themselves—in the woods
how birds see only branches, and

in the end one tree,
                    one
                            set
of deaths, chances, mistakes.
        But the birds
                        did not tell
me this, and the list
                    stretched

around the greater part of the world.
Around the greater part of the world
there is the dream of one hundred ears,
the dream of sleeping hounds…

This heat, this blue, this meaningless.

The late shade has a certainty
in its progress, in the shapes
it takes: as rooftop, as chimney.
As loud swallowing of mud,

birds, grass, trash:
                    signals
of the effable mind, the spirit
of reason. *Don't you feel*
          the stab—the elongation,
                              words
laboring inside the day?
                    The faucet

drip increases, beastly, until
nothing remains for me
but the throwing off of covers,
and then the night all around:

come in. Come in, come in, come in.

~

When I arrive back at my-
self, there is air and bathwater
between my eyes and the rest
of my body. The warm snap

ruined me,
            and now the chill
        has swung south.
Some version of this in memory
            years from now:
I was at the kitchen table,
me,
        fresh from the steam.

The storm sang about itself—
the trees trembling, again.
*What was it you wanted
to tell me? What?* Listen:

there is a cricket in the snow.

Thicket

The dog's head swells
with a mess of stars and cloud.
When he shifts, boulderlike
in his dream, the blaze-red tops
of trees now inked, he
turns the mass in long circles
that spiral and glow for hours, slow
only as he wakes—
the master is tapping his boots,
turning pages like
a deer picking through autumn frost:

as long as there is
the mountain's body for mist to sink
upward from into fine rain

as long as the animals
of the house know voices and smells
know the shadow of this roof

as long as an eye peering
outward fixes focus on itself in the glass
and the body takes one step inward

as long
as the nightblack leaves rise and fold
in us

Blackworm

Upon intrusion, the body-dark
room asks *who is this?*

I was one melody then
another, backward as treason,

one memory and cold ashes.
The room (little capitol) was

overturned: hearth tiles
cracked, the gnosis of shelves

undone and the asking still
reeling like a water-

spout over dank fathoms.
I was a list beginning

with the sea, and my name an
aberration in the list's cellar,

leaking out along
the fringes of other rooms—

you breach, you sleeping key.
I was thwarted and yet I am

the towns and their beyonds:
silent acre upon silent acre.

Vesper Inquiry

The dumb layer of leaves—
hot red and yellow going peat black
between the snow and the lawn:
a sign of the dead increasing
every second in every corner
of the body, house and town?
Must night begin always with one
of something:
                        lingering milk
of onions, ice-choked street,
swarm of banjo notes—
the silk-thin glow of clocktower
beneath aching constellations?
The breath works so long at unity
that the tree's branches are
a collective insult, and thick sleep—
a whole day of it: the stasis
of bed adrift in the room
beneath the anchorage of eye.

The body has been on the ground,
has been in flight—a thing
to be taken down by grace
and pushed off
                        into gold current
running fast with winter melt
from the path where sight turns
along each mythic neck of water
expecting the uprush of birds
where only the air ripples: sweet
threat, sting of wind's greeting.

Inaugural Visions

Some old steam went down the riverbed.
The woodpecker is a dead woman.
One view of the cosmos shows me glee.
Two pheasants tangle with a sapling pine.
I put a curse on the dog and left.
A hammer under the floor springs roots.
One view of the cosmos shows me rot.
I swear the emerald mountain moved.
In several ways, the fields are all alive.
The name of the bobwhite is its sound.
My pinecone roof is sturdy still in winter.
I saw my eyebrows pushing at the river.
The dog put a curse on me, then vomited.
A raccoon fell down the chimney and burned.
My sweaters all fly up in loose threads.
One view of the sky shows me blisters.
The forest echoes with soil blinking.
My door is eating slowly away at its edge.
The world put a curse on me and laughed.
I swear the range of sadness widens.
The opossums are all hapless widowers.
A farm two roads over smoked itself down.
Old bottles in the woods love the mud.
I've thought about kneeling near the stream.
One view of the cosmos shows me two roads.
The stove coughs red into the morning.
Last summer was the time of wellsprings.
Three crows are shitting on the woodpile.
My long hair was my own lightning.
Froth flooded to greet me at the stoop.

The color of a frog blends with the ferns.
I put a curse on the dead woman and wept.
I saw seven bats veering in the snow.
My house weighs ten times more in spring.
One view of the cosmos shows me light.
My long, windy life finds an empty den.
The hawk that spiraled down was an angel.

Winter Notice

Dear Ancestor: the songbirds of my abdomen
turn rebel—each foot I plant
splits their legs a little, just enough
to hurt them. Several times a day
the humans pour black water
down their gullets, mutter niceties
about the hell-red leaves overhead.

While they are counting
I feel the planet lean toward sleep,
steep angle facing downward.

～

When you feel the street slither
under with cold, twist your thoughts
back like lids,
               let just the music slide
under your endless sighs and words.

Take refuge
in the confusion of coffee shops,
      the layering

of liquid on grain on intestine,
and the gritting away of whitening.

Take refuge and hold back the snow.

～

Dear Ancestor: the birds outside me
peel and cluster, ready for some move
or another. This pond-sized island of rock
in the corn—something
tore the stalks up, leveled the view
I had from here. The rattle I hear
from everywhere, what the people
have busied themselves with:
the chain on each wheel
      a charm against death.

Fire: Side

So many centers to the world,
so may wire-hot wings tossing
in the stone lung of each edifice—
the nightscape is of peach-glow

windows, of pitch against them.
In the creel of light I roast
my heels, let thoughts of weather
roll back untouched, unthought—

so many coelacanths basking
in the sunless, purpled valleys,
so many teeth spat into rainwater,
so many terns hunkered tight

on sands above the waves' hiss,
so much blood hauling every
way, everywhere, that if grasses
rose to construct a net to all

veins, all creatures striving second
on second, the world would be
entangled, beautiful, and I,
with knowledge, would be alone—

the one who studies the length
of flame's duration, the one
feeding it oaks, who trusts it
in his home, stranger that it is.

Thicket

The hound I sought to rescue
in my sleep became
a black bear cub, heavy
at the border of death.
So I lifted him.

The hall is long—darkest
cherry. The hall
and its picture window we pass

and pass: the sky flushed gray,
its canopy of storm.
The cub flexes his backbone
for a moment—thing
of bones covered in fur
growing brighter in my arms
for a moment, the menace

of a white, floor-length beard
flying through me like the snow.
Darker and brighter: the window
and its view once more: winter
tossed up by floodlights
from the medic we will never find.

Waiting Turn

From where chaos centers itself,
night wheels on toward sunlight,
the brass magnitude of dawn like

a broken door turned on its side
by an intruder interested only
in the abandoned house's dead bottles

and curdling jars: where dust and moss
thicken to once more start a forest
through floorboards and crossbeams

in spite of the gushing turnpike
from which the house is seen
slouched into its green embankment,

from which the eyes of travelers
swoop back into themselves, imagining
the wind and blades of light

piercing the kitchen's disrepair,
never for once considering
how a person could arrive and stop

to touch gravel not moved in years,
wrestle the door from its last hinge and
with an empty box, step into the dark.

Captiva

*"To add something to the truth
only subtracts from the truth."*

     —a fortune cookie

But what if a thing is added
around the truth, in that halo
of forms: the twelve animals
lurching in vivid procession
from the dark? What if a sprig
of mint springs near the goat's
cloven foot? And the sharp
eye of the rabbit rotates,
the dragon's hooks of smoke
curl away, the bull's weapons
glint like palm fronds in rain,
the snake's sleek body a whip-
like lightning through clouds?

The cat hunkers back into
its honed loneliness, the grasses
spreading green beneath it.
A crowing finds itself late
in the rooster's dim belly.
The rat invents a passageway
to crawl through, and the dogs
chasing the bear through woods
create those woods, and thereby
a meadow, farmland following
where the pig cools deep in mud,
the lion panting a continent
away in the sway of shade.

And so: the world awakes.
The mountains and oceans
locked by time, their motions
across the planet like pains
through the body, and so we have
the bodies that build houses
and dams, wagons, bridges
and tunnels: the unexplainable
lit with possibility, smog-stench
of happiness, each mind circling
back to its eventual need, crass
tenderness: that thoughtless
human thoughtfulness.

The truth must be crossed
like sand, shifting where
the tides dwell. Premorning:
the green dream of land
on the Gulf's sharp horizon
where there is none, only
the blue seam, out of which
all lights and their habits
seem to emerge, the vacuum
of weather. We walked
last night in the rain.
I felt the island breathing
like a feeling around us.

About the Author

F. Daniel Rzicznek's previous collections of poetry include *Neck of the World* (winner of the 2007 May Swenson Poetry Award from Utah State University Press) and *Cloud Tablets* (winner of a Wick Poetry Center Chapbook Award). He is also coeditor, with Gary L. McDowell, of *The Rose Metal Press Field Guide to Prose Poetry: Contemporary Poets in Discussion and Practice*, forthcoming from Rose Metal Press in 2010. His poems have appeared in journals such as *Boston Review*, *The New Republic*, *Orion*, *Gray's Sporting Journal*, *The Iowa Review*, and elsewhere. He currently teaches English at Bowling Green State University in Bowling Green, Ohio.

Photograph of the author by Amanda McGuire. Used by permission.

Free Verse Editions

Edited by Jon Thompson

2009

Divination Machine by F. Daniel Rzicznek
Blood Orbits by Ger Killeen
Under the Quick by Molly Bendall
Poem from above the Hill & Selected Work by Ashur Etwebi, translated by Brenda Hillman and Diallah Haidar

2008

Quarry by Carolyn Guinzio
Between the Twilight and the Sky by Jennie Neighbors
The Prison Poems by Miguel Hernández,
   translated by Michael Smith
remanence by Boyer Rickel
What Stillness Illuminated by Yermiyahu Ahron Taub

2007

Child in the Road by Cindy Savett
Verge by Morgan Lucas Schuldt
The Flying House by Dawn-Michelle Baude

2006

Physis by Nicolas Pesque, translated by Cole Swensen
Puppet Wardrobe by Daniel Tiffany
These Beautiful Limits by Thomas Lisk
The Wash by Adam Clay

2005

A Map of Faring by Peter Riley
Signs Following by Ger Killeen
Winter Journey [Viaggio d'inverno] by Attilio Bertolucci,
   translated by Nicholas Benson